SERIES TITLES

RENAISSANCE EUROPE
was created and produced by McRae Books Srl
Via del Salviatino, 1 — 50016 — Fiesole
(Florence), (Italy)
info@mcraebooks.com
www.mcraebooks.com

Publishers: Anne McRae, Marco Nardi
Series Editor: Anne McRae
Author: Neil Grant
Main Illustrations: Andrea Morandi p. 15; Francesca
D'Ottavi pp. 29, 38–39; MM comunicazione (Manuela
Cappon, Monica Favilli) pp. 9, 33, 40–43, 44–45;
Paola Ravaglia pp. 20, 35; Claudia Saraceni pp. 16,
18–19, 26–27; Sergio pp. 10–11, 24–25
Illustrations: Studio Stalio (Alessandro Cantucci,
Fabiano Fabbrucci, Margherita Salvadori)
Maps: M. Paola Baldanzi
Photos: Bridgeman Art Library, London/Alinari Photo
Library, Florence pp. 40–41b; ©Marka/Brännhage 36–37;
Mondadori Electa, Milan 32tl; Scala Archives, Florence
pp. 6b, 6tr, 12c, 13l, 15t, 23b, 26tc, 30–31, 31tr;
Art Director: Marco Nardi
Layouts: Starry Dog Books Ltd
Project Editor: Loredana Agosta
Research: Valerie Meek, Claire Moore
Editing: Tall Tree Ltd, London
Repro: Litocolor, Florence

Consultant:

Dr. Ronald Fritze is a historian of early modern
Europe and England. He is the author of *New Worlds:
The Great Voyages of OF Discovery* (Sutton/Praeger,
2003). He appeared on the History Channel series
The Conquest of America and is a member of the
Society for the History of Discoveries. Currently he
is beginning work on a brief biography of
Christopher Columbus.

Library of Congress Cataloging-in-Publication Data

Grant, Neil, 1938-
  Renaissance Europe / Neil Grant.
      p. cm. -- (History of the world)
  Summary: "A detailed overview of the history of
Europe during the fourteenth and fifteenth centuries,
when the cultural movement known as the
Renaissance made great advances in intellectual and
artistic traditions"--Provided by publisher.
  Includes index.
  ISBN 978-8860981530
  1. Renaissance--Juvenile literature. 2. Civilization,
Medieval--Juvenile literature. 3. Europe--History--
476-1492--Juvenile literature. 4. Europe--History--
1492-1648--Juvenile literature. I. Title.
  CB361.G73 2009
  940.2--dc22
                                      2008008408

Printed and bound in Malaysia.

HISTORY

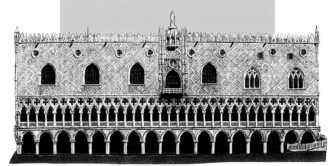

Renaissance Europe

Neil Grant

Consultant: Dr. Ronald H. Fritze, Dean of Arts and Sciences,
Professor of History, Athens State University, Alabama

Zak
BOOKS

Contents

A detail of the painting, The Four Apostles (1526) by Albrecht Dürer (1471–1528). It bears quotations from the German translation of the Bible.

TIMELINE

	1400	1425	1450	1475
 **ITALY**	The Medici family bank is founded in Florence.	Brunelleschi begins work on the dome of Florence Cathedral.	The Council of Florence brings scholars from eastern Europe to Italy.	The Sforzas rule Milan.	Leon Battista Alberti publishes the first printed book on architecture.
 **ROME AND THE PAPACY**		Martin V becomes the first pope after the Great Schism.		Papacy of Nicholas V, patron of art and literature.	During the papacy of Sixtus IV large building projects are paid for by high taxes.
 **SPAIN AND PORTUGAL**					Ferdinand of Aragon and Isabella of Castile rule Spain.
GERMANY AND THE LOW COUNTRIES		The International Gothic style is established; rise of Dutch/Flemish painting.		Jan van Eyck paints the portrait of Giovanni Arnolfini and his wife.	
 **FRANCE**					Charles VIII becomes king of France.
ENGLAND AND SCOTLAND					William Caxton sets up the first English printing press.
CENTRAL AND EASTERN EUROPE		Ottoman Turks make significant conquests in south-east Europe.		The Turks conquer Constantinople, ending the Byzantine Empire.	

Introduction

I n the 19th century, scholars began using the term "Renaissance" to explain the great flowering of culture that took place in Europe in the 14th and 15th centuries. This was the movement that launched the intellectual and artistic traditions of today's world. Yet the conditions in which the Renaissance first flourished were very unpromising. The continent was ravaged by long periods of warfare, the Church was deeply divided, and plague was destroying whole populations. Despite this, Europe made a comeback, mainly as a result of trade. Sea and land routes linked the continent, spreading money, goods and also new ideas. Newly rich city-states in Italy, where the ruins of classical civilisation were still standing, used their wealth to imitate the glory of the Roman Empire itself. Their artists condemned the recent "dark age" and set their minds to reviving the spirit of the classical past.

A detail of a painting titled The Ambassadors *(1533) by the German painter Hans Holbein the Younger (1497–1543), portrays a typical Renaissance man, surrounded by books and scientific instruments.*

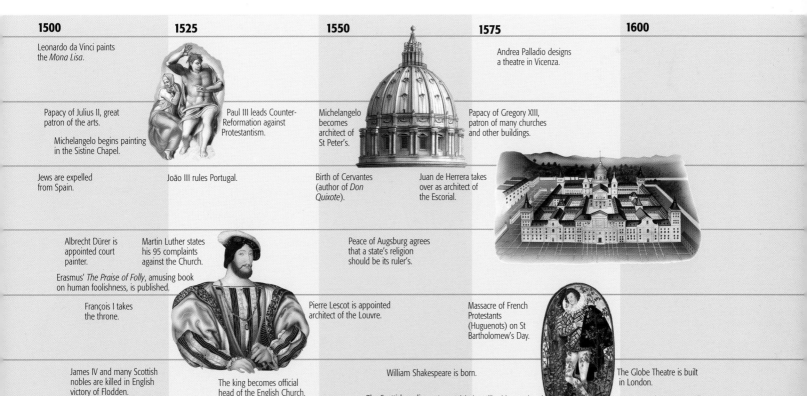

1500	1525	1550	1575	1600
Leonardo da Vinci paints the *Mona Lisa*.			Andrea Palladio designs a theatre in Vicenza.	
Papacy of Julius II, great patron of the arts.	Paul III leads Counter-Reformation against Protestantism.	Michelangelo becomes architect of St Peter's.	Papacy of Gregory XIII, patron of many churches and other buildings.	
Michelangelo begins painting in the Sistine Chapel.				
Jews are expelled from Spain.	João III rules Portugal.	Birth of Cervantes (author of *Don Quixote*).	Juan de Herrera takes over as architect of the Escorial.	
Albrecht Dürer is appointed court painter.	Martin Luther states his 95 complaints against the Church.	Peace of Augsburg agrees that a state's religion should be its ruler's.		
Erasmus' *The Praise of Folly*, amusing book on human foolishness, is published.				
François I takes the throne.		Pierre Lescot is appointed architect of the Louvre.	Massacre of French Protestants (Huguenots) on St Bartholomew's Day.	
James IV and many Scottish nobles are killed in English victory of Flodden.	The king becomes official head of the English Church.	William Shakespeare is born.		The Globe Theatre is built in London.
		The Scottish parliament adopts Calvinism.	Nicholas Hillard is appointed court miniaturist.	Inigo Jones studies ancient buildings in Rome.
	Gustavus Vasa escapes from Danish prison and launches revolt.	Ivan IV ("the Terrible") becomes tsar of Russia.	Poland and Lithuania agree on formal union.	End of the Livonian war: Latvia and Estonia are divided between Poland, Lithuania and Sweden.

The Decline of the Middle Ages

For people living in 14th-century Europe life had hardly changed in hundreds of years. A peasant lived and worked where he was born. He owed loyalty to his lord, who in turn served a greater lord, and so on up to the king. The other authority was the Church, headed by the pope, which dictated people's beliefs and behavior. But huge changes were on the way. Bonds of service were replaced by payments in cash wages. Countries became nation-states, ruled by ambitious kings. Doubts about the old religion were part of a new spirit of curiosity, which also led to the revival of scholarship.

Details (here and below) of the fresco cycle painted by the Italian artist Benozzo Gozzoli (1420–1497) in the Medici palace in Florence. The artist may have been inspired by the procession of eastern scholars that came to Florence in 1439.

The fall of Constantinople, painted in 1499. The style is Medieval, rather than Renaissance.

Portrait of the Italian poet Giovanni Boccaccio (1313–1375). Both he and Petrarch laid the foundations of Renaissance literature.

Seeds of the Renaissance

At first, the word "renaissance" meant the revival of the learning of ancient Greece and Rome, which, being non-Christian, was not encouraged by the Church. The revival began in northern Italy. A key figure was the poet Francesco Petrarca, known as Petrarch (1304–1374), who believed that the ancients commanded "all wisdom and rules of right conduct".

The Fall of Constantinople

In 1453, the Ottoman Turks (who were Muslims) captured Constantinople, the 1,000-year-old home of Eastern Orthodox Christianity. Greek-speaking scholars fled to the West with ancient writings unknown in Italy, helping to advance the new learning of the Renaissance.

EUROPE IN 1400

SCOTLAND, ENGLAND, BRUGES, FRANCE, PORTUGAL, CASTILE, HOLY ROMAN EMPIRE, POLAND-LITHUANIA, HUNGARY, FLORENCE, PAPAL STATES, OTTOMAN EMPIRE, CONSTANTINOPLE

Hapsburg territories — Boundary of the Holy Roman Empire

Europe After the Black Death

In 1400 Europe was still suffering the effects of plague. Farming and trade were badly damaged, workers were few, and discontent led to rebellions and wars. The old Holy Roman Empire, which ruled with the backing of the pope, had control over most of Europe. But powerful new nation-states were emerging, especially those of France, England and Spain. Meanwhile, the Turks threatened Eastern Europe.

War and Disease

The 14th century was a miserable time. Violence was common. Rival princes fought to control France, Italian states clashed, there were frequent peasant uprisings and the authority of the Church was badly damaged by political struggles. Worst of all, one-third of Europe's population died of the Black Death, an epidemic plague.

The Rise of Towns

With feudal society breaking down, more peasants worked for wages and paid their rent in cash. Kings who had relied upon their subjects to provide their armies now hired mercenaries. As trade grew along with banking, so did towns, especially in Italy and the Low Countries.

Typical Renaissance houses in Bruges, present-day Belgium.

This illustration shows the English defeat of an invading French fleet off the port of Sluys (in present-day Holland), in 1340.

Early Renaissance Italy

The Renaissance was the period between the Middle Ages and the Modern Era. It was a time when the ancient learning of Greece and Rome was rediscovered, and new ideas about art, religion and science thrived. The Renaissance began in northern Italy in the early 1300s. Nowhere was it stronger than in Florence, a city that had grown wealthy from trade. There, princes and trade guilds commissioned new art and architecture, and created a culture than soon began to spread across Europe.

View of 14th-century Florence.

Portrait of Lorenzo de' Medici.

Florence

Florence was the "queen" of the early Renaissance. It was the home of humanists such as Boccaccio (the "father" of Italian prose), Dante Alighieri (1265–1321) and the painter Giotto di Bondone (1266–1337). The city set the standards in art and learning. Nothing like the cathedral of the architect Filippo Brunelleschi (1377–1446) had been seen in Europe since ancient times. The humanist academy of Marsilio Ficino (1433–1499) combined classical learning with Christian thought.

The Medici

In 1434, Cosimo de' Medici (1389–1464), head of a powerful merchant family, gained control of the republic of Florence. For the next three centuries the history of Florence is the history of the Medici. Cosimo's grandson Lorenzo ("the Magnificent," 1449–1492) was a brilliant Renaissance prince, cultured and clever. A generous patron, he encouraged artists such as Michelangelo Buonarroti (1475–1564).

Guilds and Merchants

Guilds were medieval associations for the members of trades and professions, ranging from merchants and lawyers to bakers and fishmongers. They protected their members' interests and ensured good production standards. Wealthy guilds supported religious charities and sponsored artists' competitions. Some were powerful in city politics.

Crowds listen to a preacher in Siena, northern Italy. Siena was an early center of Renaissance culture that influenced its larger neighbor, Florence.

Italian States

Italy during the 15th century comprised more than a dozen rival kingdoms, duchies, and republics. The largest territorially was the Kingdom of Naples, which occupied most of Italy's southern mainland. In the center, the pope controlled the territories surrounding Rome. To the north, the main powers were the republic of Florence and the Duchy of Milan. The republic of Venice controlled the Aegean Sea.

—— *Border of the Holy Roman Empire*

ITALY IN THE 15TH CENTURY

DUCHY OF SAVOY
REPUBLIC OF VENICE
DUCHY OF MILAN
REPUBLIC OF FLORENCE
REPUBLIC OF GENOA
PISA • SIENA • FLORENCE
PAPAL STATES
REPUBLIC OF SIENA
• ROME
AEGEAN SEA
KINGDOM OF NAPLES
KINGDOM OF ARAGON

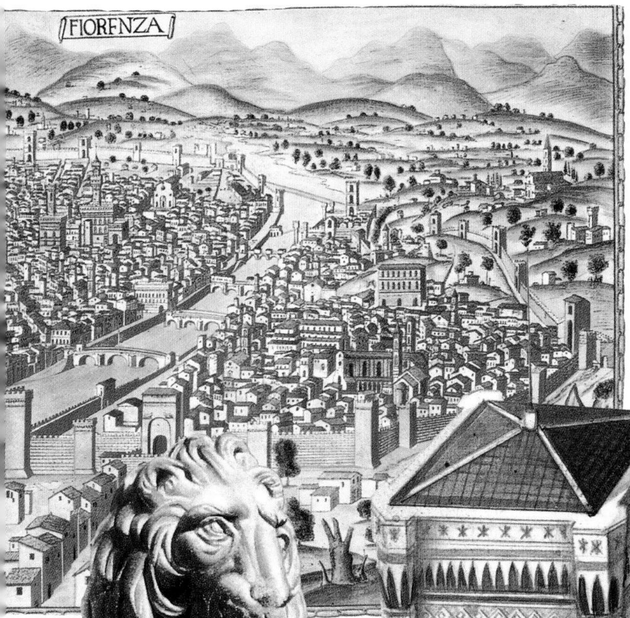

A Florentine guild commissioned the bronze doors of the cathedral's baptistry from Lorenzo Ghiberti (1378–1455). This panel depicts the sacrifice of Isaac.

Civic Pride

The northern Italian city-states were independent. Many governed themselves democratically during the Middle Ages, although by the time of the Renaissance power was usually held by a small wealthy class. Most citizens were very proud of their city, and took part in colorful ceremonies that expressed civic pride. The city's success made them rich, and both individuals and governments liked to display their importance through fine new buildings and works of art.

The dome of Florence's cathedral, shown here, took 14 years to complete.

Sculpture of the lion, symbol of the city of Florence.

EVENTS IN ITALY

1397
The Medici family bank is founded in Florence.

1399
The communal governments of Siena and Pisa surrender their cities into the hands of Giangaleazzo Visconti (1351–1402), Duke of Milan.

1421
Brunelleschi begins work on the dome of Florence Cathedral.

1424
Ghiberti finishes his first set of bronze doors (north doors) for the baptistry of Florence.

1447
The end of the Visconti Dynasty, rulers of Milan since 1277; they are followed (1450) by the Sforza.

Antiquity and Humanism

HUMANISM

1324
The poet Petrarch begins collecting ancient Latin manuscripts.

1362
Classical Greek texts by Homer (8th century BCE) and Euripides (died 406 BCE) are translated into Latin and published in Florence.

1419
Scholar Poggio Bracciolini (1380–1459) discovers many classical texts.

1460
English scholars visit Italy and learn Greek.

1462
Humanist thinker Marcilio Ficino becomes head of the Platonic Academy in Florence.

1470
First printing press set up in Paris. Greek classics are printed in Latin.

1486
Ancient Roman textbook on the principles of classical architecture by Vitruvius published.

For a thousand years nearly all learning and art in Europe was centred in the Christian Church. The ancient civilizations of Greece and Rome, which existed before Christianity, were not forgotten but were little known. Gradually, however, the learning of the ancients was rediscovered. Greek works were studied, as were Arabic translations of lost Greek originals. This interest in learning inspired people to think for themselves, and the Renaissance was a time of rapid advance in all kinds of knowledge. The early Renaissance thinkers are called "humanists" because they were deeply interested in questions about human beings and the world around them—questions for which the Church had only theological answers.

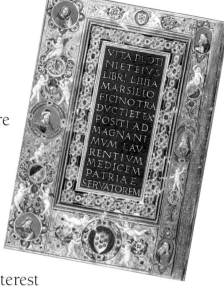

Early printed books were beautifully made. This page is from a book by the humanist philosopher and teacher, Marsilio Ficino.

The Dutch scholar Desiderius Erasmus (1469–1536), who travelled to many countries, was Europe's voice of tolerance, humor and good sense.

The illustration below shows a bookcase from the library of the Duke of Urbino. A Renaissance patron such as the duke would have used his library often. It was not just for show.

Libraries

Before the invention of printing, books were rare and expensive, but with the new interest in learning, many rich men assembled libraries. Books were in Latin, the language of ancient Rome, which all educated people understood. Yet it was the Greeks who were the true founders of classical civilization, and few people could read Greek. (The Vatican library had only three Greek books in 1447.) A century later, most humanist scholars knew Greek, and most Greek works had been translated into Latin.

European Humanists

Humanists were not against religion or, at first, the Church. They hoped to combine Christian and classical values. Although humanism began in Italy, humanist scholars soon emerged in other countries, including the most famous, Erasmus (Dutch), and his many friends, such as Thomas More (English, 1477–1535), John Colet (English, 1477–1519), and Guillaume Budé (French, 1467–1540).

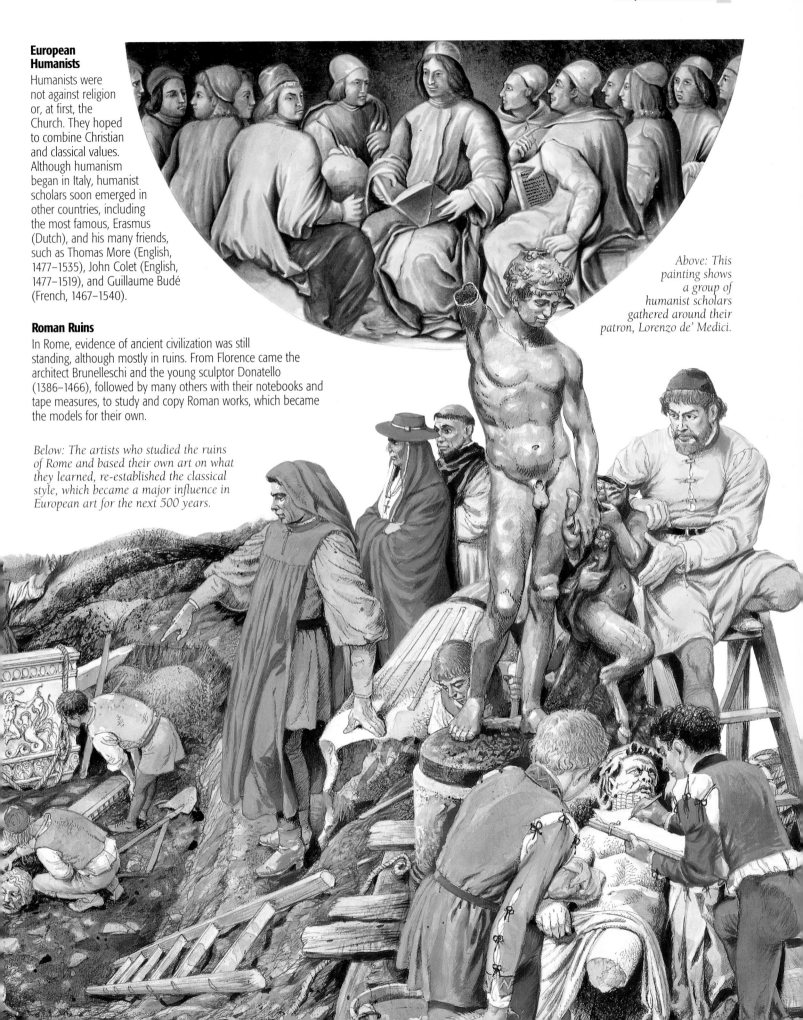

Above: This painting shows a group of humanist scholars gathered around their patron, Lorenzo de' Medici.

Roman Ruins

In Rome, evidence of ancient civilization was still standing, although mostly in ruins. From Florence came the architect Brunelleschi and the young sculptor Donatello (1386–1466), followed by many others with their notebooks and tape measures, to study and copy Roman works, which became the models for their own.

Below: The artists who studied the ruins of Rome and based their own art on what they learned, re-established the classical style, which became a major influence in European art for the next 500 years.

Early Renaissance Art

When Italian artists and sculptors began imitating the ancient masters their work represented a break with the Medieval past. For the first time since antiquity, artists learned the skills needed to present people and objects in a convincing and naturalistic way. The discovery of the rules of perspective was a major breakthrough. Religious subjects in art still dominated, but there was now also a growing interest in secular subjects.

Influence of Classical Art

Although artists often "borrowed" exact details from classical Roman works, from about 1450 they began to understand the principles on which these works were made. Blind imitation was easy enough. Far more difficult and more important was to learn the techniques used by the ancients to achieve astonishingly life-like works of art.

Donatello's David (1434) was the first nude sculpture since antiquity.

Detail from a painting by Botticelli titled The Spring, *showing the mythological figures known as* The Three Graces.

The Florentine artist Sandro Botticelli (1445–1510) completed this altarpiece, The Annunciation, *for a family chapel in 1490. It still has its original frame.*

Altarpieces

The Church remained an important patron of art in the early Renaissance, and some of its biggest commissions were altarpieces (the decorative backing for an altar). An altarpiece may consist of a single painting, or, more often, a group of paintings, often with carving or sculpture. Sometimes more than one artist worked on one over several years.

Early Renaissance Painters

The painter's range of subject-matter increased enormously. Renaissance artists, like the ancient Greeks, were interested in humanity, and it became possible again to represent the human nude. To the familiar images of Christianity, the Renaissance added classical history and mythology. Artists themselves moved up the social scale. Formerly mere craftsmen, like carpenters, fine artists became admired celebrities.

The Trinity (1427), a fresco by Masaccio (1401–1428), one of the greatest early Florentine masters. The stunning use of perspective makes the arch look real, an effect that caused a sensation at the time.

Masaccio has used a technique called foreshortening to give the barrel-vaulted ceiling an appearance of depth.

Perspective

The aim of both classical and Renaissance art and sculpture was realism. In painting, realism faced a particular problem: how to represent a scene, which is in three dimensions, on a flat surface, which has only two. Solving the technical problems of representing depth, or perspective, fascinated early Renaissance artists. An artist might paint, for example, a street scene, just to show off his command of perspective.

Right: An artist sketches using a grid. This helps him depict the subject's true proportions.

John the Baptist and the Virgin stand before God, who is supporting the crucified Jesus.

The wife of Lorenzo Leni, who commissioned the work, is shown as a humble supplicant before the altar.

Leni himself kneels outside the painted architectural scene. His face and folding gown are realistic and subtle.

Portraits

Another revived subject was the portrait. By the late 15th century, princes and merchants wanted portraits of themselves. Artists also did self-portraits, and used friends as models. Some art patrons had their portraits included in the works they commissioned. Many Renaissance paintings of religious subjects include portraits of the wealthy patrons alongside figures of Christ, the Madonna or the saints, as in The Trinity (above left).

Detail from a fresco (1459) by Gozzoli in which the painter himself (with name on cap) appears with members of the Medici family.

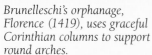

Brunelleschi's orphanage, Florence (1419), uses graceful Corinthian columns to support round arches.

The Pazzi Chapel by Brunelleschi, Florence (1429), uses a grand, Roman-style arch. The small dome on top suggests a Roman temple.

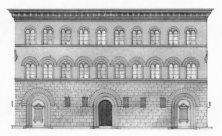

Bartolommeo's fortress-like Medici palace, Florence (1444), surrounds a colonnaded courtyard similar to those of Roman villas.

Alberti's Church of Santa Maria Novella, Florence (1470), uses a harmonious classical façade.

Alberti's Church of Sant' Andrea (c. 1470), in Mantua, is a reinvention of a Roman triumphal arch.

Early Renaissance Architecture

Brunelleschi, the first Renaissance architect, began as a sculptor and goldsmith. It was his study of ancient Roman buildings that made him turn to architecture. The Renaissance style that began with him, and that has influenced Western architects ever since, was based on that of ancient Rome, which was, of course, native to Italy. But in time the new style spread across Europe, where Roman remains were less common. The Renaissance style was not completely new, nor completely Roman. It was an adaptation. Architects may be influenced by an earlier age, but cannot repeat it. Romans built public baths, amphitheaters, and temples. The new age required churches, palaces, and villas.

Renaissance Style

The two great pioneers of Renaissance architecture were Brunelleschi and Alberti. Brunelleschi was a hands-on, old-style, master-builder, whereas Alberti was a scholar who designed buildings to be built by others. Brunelleschi's buildings have the classical virtues of harmony and order, and details such as carved capitals on columns are essentially Roman. Alberti's few buildings show his gift for reinventing ancient forms, and his book, *De re aedificatoria* ("Ten Books on Architecture", 1452), became the manual for Renaissance architects.

Brunelleschi

Brunelleschi's cathedral dome in Florence (1434) is thought to mark the beginning of Renaissance architecture. One domed building from the ancient world survived in the form of the Pantheon, in Rome, which Brunelleschi studied. However, his own dome owes more to the style of Gothic (Medieval) architecture than it does to ancient Rome. But he deserves his reputation as a founder of the Renaissance style for his other buildings, such as the Foundlings' Hospital, or orphanage, the Medici church of San Lorenzo and the Pazzi Chapel.

Brunelleschi's dome uses a formula found in pointed stone arches (used to support heavy Medieval roofs), which Gothic builders knew but ancient Romans did not.

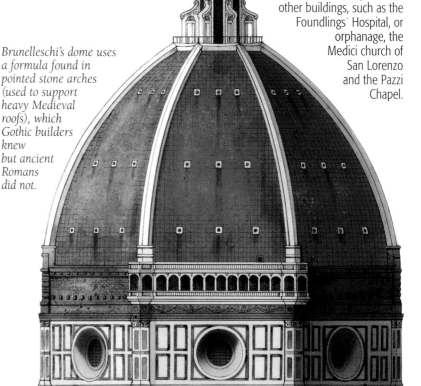

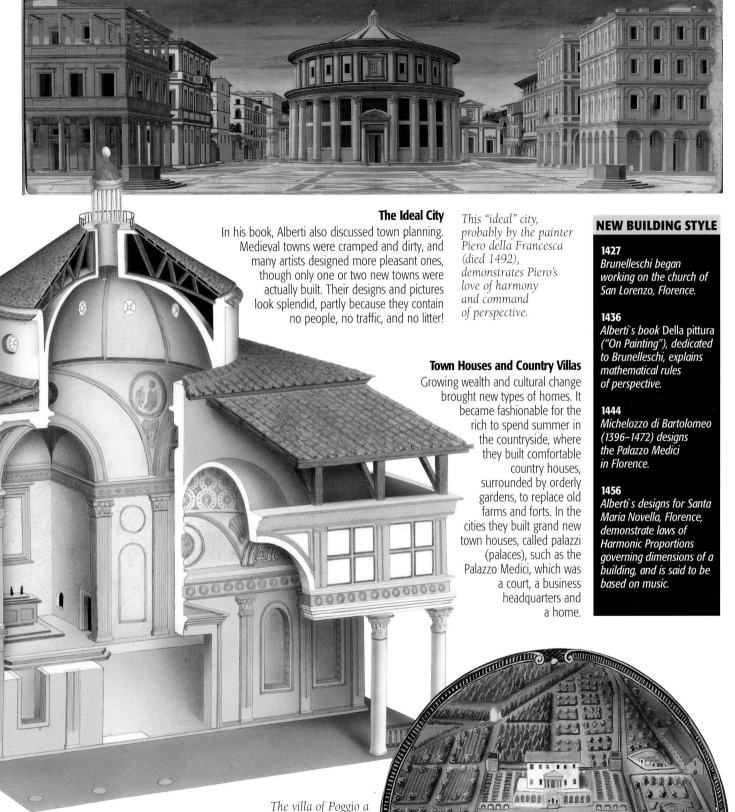

The Ideal City

In his book, Alberti also discussed town planning. Medieval towns were cramped and dirty, and many artists designed more pleasant ones, though only one or two new towns were actually built. Their designs and pictures look splendid, partly because they contain no people, no traffic, and no litter!

This "ideal" city, probably by the painter Piero della Francesca (died 1492), demonstrates Piero's love of harmony and command of perspective.

Town Houses and Country Villas

Growing wealth and cultural change brought new types of homes. It became fashionable for the rich to spend summer in the countryside, where they built comfortable country houses, surrounded by orderly gardens, to replace old farms and forts. In the cities they built grand new town houses, called palazzi (palaces), such as the Palazzo Medici, which was a court, a business headquarters and a home.

NEW BUILDING STYLE

1427
Brunelleschi began working on the church of San Lorenzo, Florence.

1436
Alberti's book Della pittura *("On Painting"), dedicated to Brunelleschi, explains mathematical rules of perspective.*

1444
Michelozzo di Bartolomeo (1396–1472) designs the Palazzo Medici in Florence.

1456
Alberti's designs for Santa Maria Novella, Florence, demonstrate laws of Harmonic Proportions governing dimensions of a building, and is said to be based on music.

A cut-away illustration showing the interior of Brunelleschi's Renaissance masterpiece, the Pazzi Chapel.

The villa of Poggio a Caiano, country home of Lorenzo de' Medici, was designed by Giuliano da Sangallo (1445–1516), a follower of Brunelleschi, c. 1482.

Printing and Education

The Renaissance could not have happened without one revolutionary new invention: printing with moveable metal type. For the first time, books could be mass-produced easily and cheaply. Medieval books were written by hand. Making a single copy took months, so books were rare and precious. Knowledge in Medieval Europe was spread slowly by word of mouth through church sermons and travelers' gossip. Now printed books could carry the ideas of the humanists to every town, court, and university within weeks.

Gutenberg's Invention

Printing with wooden blocks had been practised in Europe from about 1400. It was slow: a wood block took time to cut, and then made only one page in one book. Many craftsmen were trying other methods, but the man who probably printed the first book from moveable type was Johannes Gutenberg (died 1468) of Mainz, Germany, in about 1455.

The Printing Press

To make each letter, or type, Gutenberg cut it into a bronze slab, from which he could make many casts in molten metal. Type was put together in a frame to form an image of a single page (in reverse). It was coated with ink and pressed on to a sheet of paper. Many copies could be made one after another. Then the next page was composed. Gutenberg also developed a special ink, which would stick to metal. He modelled his press on a wine press.

1

The typecaster makes each type by pouring molten metal into a copper cast.

2

The compositor sets the type into a tray and wedges it securely with wooden blocks. Next, the type is dabbed in ink and the paper pinned on top.

Schools and Universities

The thirst for knowledge led to a growth in universities and great changes in education. Medieval teaching was run by the Church, which taught subjects such as grammar and rhetoric. The revival of ancient learning, especially philosophy, and the spread of humanism, breathed new life into teaching.

As a rule, only boys (no girls) from rich families went to school.

The first books published are not easy to read today. They were typeset in a Medieval Gothic font similar to the writing style used by monks.

A piece of individual moveable type was called a sort. A good typecaster could make 4,000 sorts a day.

THE SPREAD OF PRINTING IN EUROPE

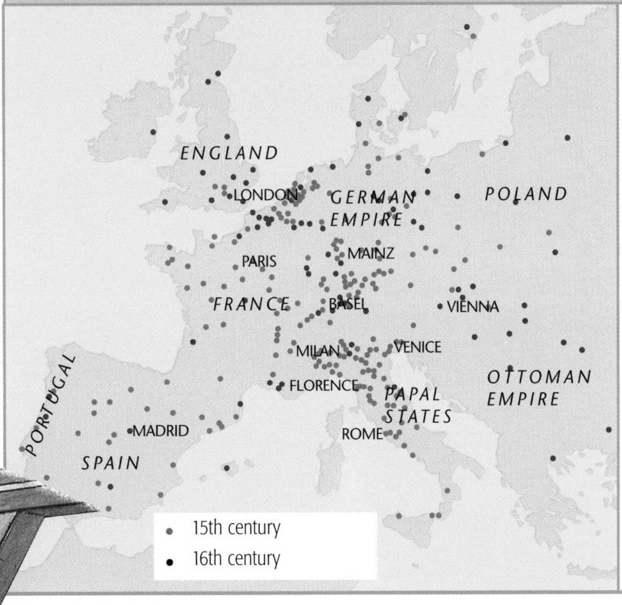

ENGLAND

LONDON

GERMAN EMPIRE

POLAND

PARIS

MAINZ

FRANCE

BASEL

VIENNA

MILAN

VENICE

FLORENCE

PAPAL STATES

OTTOMAN EMPIRE

PORTUGAL

MADRID

ROME

SPAIN

- 15th century
- 16th century

Printing Centers

This map shows the centers of European printing during the Renaissance. The speed with which printing spread shows that the breakthrough in technology might have happened anywhere, and that the most "advanced" regions, northern Italy and the Low Countries, had the most printers.

3

The press, or "platen" is brought down on the paper to make an impression and the sheets are sent to dry.

4

The printed sheets are sorted into the correct order. Finally they are sewn with linen thread and fitted into a vellum cover.

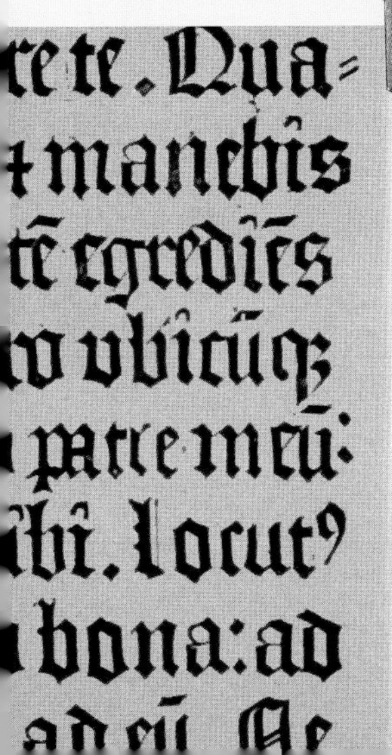

Books and Reading

Printing spread rapidly. Printed books were expensive, but much cheaper than manuscripts. Many people could afford to buy them, and more people learned to read. New libraries were founded and old ones expanded. Early books were on religion, philosophy, and law, but printers were soon producing poetry and stories.

After 1500, most people richer than the peasants, including women, could read and write.

Banking, Trade, and Industry

Plague, which devastated Europe's economy in 1348 and 1349, returned in later years, delaying recovery. But by 1400, there were signs of improvement. Farmland that had been abandoned was cultivated once again, and population grew. Plague and civil unrest had broken the old feudal system. Peasants, now mostly wage-earners, learned new skills. They were able to move about to find better-paid jobs. Farming methods became more efficient. Greater prosperity increased demand, not only for food but for goods and services. Trade and industry prospered.

The Florentine gold coin, the Florin, was first minted in 1252. It became the standard coinage of Europe.

From the 15th century, Venice was renowned for its superb glassmaking, an industry controlled by a powerful guild. Seen here is a Venetian glassmaker's workshop. Workers sat on small stools around the mouths of a furnace so that they could reach the molten glass inside. The glass was blown into shape then crafted with fine detail.

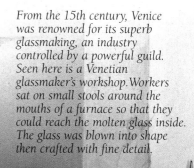

Banking

Banking was a family business. It had almost disappeared during the Middle Ages because the Church condemned money-lending. But by the 15th century, banking became well organized. The families of the Peruzzi and Bardi (and later the Medici) in Italy, and the Welsers and Fuggers in Germany, had agents in many countries. It could be a risky business. The Peruzzi and Bardi were ruined when major debtors, including the King of England, failed to pay.

A 15th-century safe with iron reinforcements from Milan.

Above: Coats of arms of some of Florence's major corporations, or guilds.

Industry

The textile industry was the largest in Europe, but, in certain places, mining, shipbuilding, or another local speciality, overtook it. Europe had no large factories, as we know them. Manufacturing took place in workshops, and although some large operations existed, a typical workshop was just part of the master-craftsman's house.

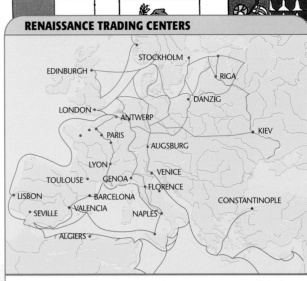

RENAISSANCE TRADING CENTERS

— Venetian routes   — Hanseatic routes   ● Town linked
— Genoese routes   ● Hanseatic center   with Antwerp

Trading Ports

Trade was the lifeblood of Europe's great ports. In the Mediterranean, Venice, and Genoa competed for the rich Eastern trade. In the Low Countries, Antwerp, which had the first stock market (1460), was a major center of the cloth trade. Seville thrived on trade with America in the 16th century. The inland port of Lyon, on the Rhone River, grew rich on exports of silk.

Merchants

Merchants, like bankers, might grow rich, or might be ruined in a moment. One shipload of goods might make a man's fortune. But if it sank at sea or was captured by pirates, he lost everything. Though not insured against loss, merchants often had some protection. The Hanseatic League, an alliance of trading ports in Northern Europe, monopolised trade in the region, won privileges for its members, and defended them against rivals.

Right: A 15th-century Italian merchant receives bad news from his agent abroad.

Imports and Exports

In long-distance trade, the main goods traded were necessities such as grain, salt, fish, metals, cloth, and wine. France, for example, exported wine to England in exchange for grain. It was difficult to export many foods unless they were preserved in some way through pickling or salting. The biggest trade was in cloth, especially from Florence and the Flemish towns. The East supplied spices and other luxuries.

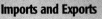

The work of peasants, such as these sheep shearers, was a fundamental part of the wool industry.

This exquisite 15th-century statue of Apollo was one of many such pieces commissioned by Isabella d'Este (see below and opposite).

Northern Italy

Great art requires not only great artists but also wealthy patrons. In the Middle Ages, the chief patron was the Church, and so religion was the subject of nearly all great art of the time. During the Renaissance, patronage came also from rich and powerful individuals, and institutions such as governments. The north Italian states, great and small, were dominated by ruling families and their courts. These privileged people delighted in showing off their wealth. Many were often intelligent and cultured men and women, who were good judges of art and artists.

Ruling Families

Princely families, like the Medici in Florence or the Sforza in Milan, were powerful political figures on the European scene as well as patrons of art and learning. But some of the greatest patrons ruled much smaller states. The Gonzagas in Mantua built a magnificent palace-museum although their state was the size of a county.

This medal commemorates a triumph of Giovanni Gonzaga (died 1444), the ruler of Mantua. Much fine art resulted from his intelligent patronage of gifted artists.

The Renaissance patroness Isabella d'Este (1474–1539) learned Latin, and had her portrait painted by the finest artists of the day.

Maritime Powers

Venice was "married" to the sea by the doge (the ruler of Venice) in a special annual ceremony, and its wealth, in fact its very existence, depended on the sea. Venice's chief rival was Genoa. Both cities had trading colonies on the Black Sea, but Genoa, on the other side of Italy, was further from the eastern trade routes, and so Venice held the advantage.

The elaborate façades of the doge's palace were completed in 1424. An upper storey of beautiful rose-colored marble surmounts arcades of Gothic arches.

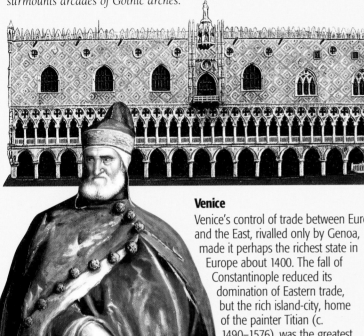

This detail, depicting the month of April, comes from a lavish fresco in the "Hall of the Months" at the Palazzo Schifanoia, in Ferrara. The palace was the summer home of the Este family.

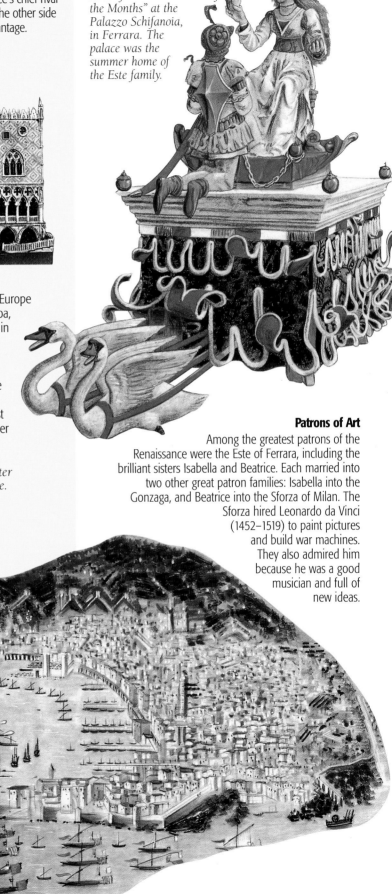

Venice

Venice's control of trade between Europe and the East, rivalled only by Genoa, made it perhaps the richest state in Europe about 1400. The fall of Constantinople reduced its domination of Eastern trade, but the rich island-city, home of the painter Titian (c. 1490–1576), was the greatest center of Renaissance art after Florence and Rome.

Portrait of the Doge Andrea Gritti, by Titian, who was also court painter to the Emperor Charles V (reigned 1519–1556), ruler of half of Europe.

Patrons of Art

Among the greatest patrons of the Renaissance were the Este of Ferrara, including the brilliant sisters Isabella and Beatrice. Each married into two other great patron families: Isabella into the Gonzaga, and Beatrice into the Sforza of Milan. The Sforza hired Leonardo da Vinci (1452–1519) to paint pictures and build war machines. They also admired him because he was a good musician and full of new ideas.

Rulers of Venice

Venice was a unique state in many ways. It was a republic, with an elected leader, the doge, who appeared to rule much like a king and held office for life. He was always a member of the aristocratic elite, and at home his powers were limited by law. The system worked well: Venice escaped the revolts and riots that shook other governments.

View of Genoa in the 15th century. Still a strong sea power, Genoa produced the greatest admiral of the Renaissance, Andrea Doria (1466–1560).

Rebellious soldiers attack the Castel Sant'Angelo, the pope's castle outside the Vatican.

Pope Julius II, the "warrior pope," painted by Raphael.

Rome and the Papacy

After the Great Schism, the papacy lost much of its authority. The Renaissance popes did little to restore its reputation. They acted more like ruling princes than religious leaders. Most were ambitious, closely involved in politics, and mainly interested in enlarging papal power and the fortunes of their families. Popes were also cultured men and strong patrons of the arts. By 1500 Rome had overtaken Florence as the leading Renaissance city.

Michelangelo's dome for St. Peter's in Rome remains an amazing feat of engineering. Paired columns surrounding the base bear the vast weight of the dome and spire.

The New Rome

During the Renaissance, the dirty, cramped old city of Rome was largely rebuilt, thanks to the popes. Nicholas V began it, restoring many public buildings. The work continued under his successors including Julius II, who built many new roads. Finally, the most ambitious plan to turn Rome into an "ideal city" was begun under one of the greatest Renaissance popes, Sixtus V.

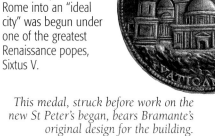

This medal, struck before work on the new St Peter's began, bears Bramante's original design for the building.

St. Peter's Basilica

By the 15th century the huge church, founded in 330 and containing the tomb of St. Peter, was in poor condition. Finally, Pope Julius II asked Bramante (1414–1514), one of the leading architects of the day, to design a new church. Bramante's plan, in the form of a Greek cross, was changed somewhat by Michelangelo, who designed the immense dome. In 1606, Carlo Maderno (1556–1629) redesigned the church as a Latin cross.

The Sack of Rome

In 1527 the soldiers of the Emperor Charles V in Italy, who had not been paid for months, attacked Rome, rampaging through the city killing, looting, and destroying. The pope fled, as did the artists, and many others. An age had ended. The heyday of Renaissance Rome was over, and the pope, like it or not, was firmly under the emperor's control.

Artists in Rome

Between about 1494 and 1527, practically every gifted artist in Italy (especially Florence) visited and worked in Rome. Leonardo da Vinci lived in an apartment in the Vatican as an old man. He painted nothing for the pope (who preferred Raphael), but was involved in engineering projects, such as draining the Pontine Marshes. He knew many people, including Michelangelo, the architects Sangallo and Bramante, and met the young Raphael (1483–1520).

Right: This detail from a fresco by Michelangelo was commissioned by Pope Julius II for the Sistine Chapel, in Rome. It depicts God creating Adam. The colorful work includes over 300 biblical figures and is among the finest works of art ever made.

Below: This fresco by Perugino, also in the Sistine Chapel, shows Christ giving the keys of the Church to St Peter. The setting displays the artist's flair for figure work and perspective.

Papal Patronage

The popes were able to attract almost any artist they wanted to Rome. The Sistine Chapel was decorated by Michelangelo (who painted the famous ceiling), Botticelli, Ghirlandaio, Perugino, and other great artists. Besides hiring Michelangelo, Pope Julius II persuaded Raphael to decorate the pope's chambers with frescoes, and appointed Bramante to begin the rebuilding of Christianity's principal church, St. Peter's Cathedral.

Spain and Portugal

In the Middle Ages much of Spain was under Muslim control, with the Christians split among several small kingdoms. After Castile and Aragon united in 1469, the rest of Spain followed. Granada, the last Muslim foothold, was conquered in 1492—the year Columbus landed in America. In 1519, Carlos I of Spain became Holy Roman Emperor Charles V, overlord of half of Europe. When Philip II became king in 1556, Spain was the greatest power in the world.

The Spanish Inquisition

Although this was Spain's "golden age," society was intolerant. The Inquisition, which began in the 13th century to fight heresy, reached Spain under the joint reign of Ferdinand of Aragon and Isabella of Castile. Jews and Muslims were considered a threat to the Church and were forced to convert to Christianity or flee. Persons accused of heresy were tried and often tortured then burned alive.

This detail from a painting by the Castilian Pedro Berruguete (c. 1450–1503) shows convicted heretics (with white hats) awaiting their sentence.

Granada: the Last Muslim Stronghold

The end of Moorish (Muslim) rule in Spain came during the reign of Muhammad XI (reigned 1482–1527), called Boabdil by the Spanish. Boabdil invaded Castile soon after becoming king but was taken prisoner. He was granted freedom by agreeing to deliver the lands held by his brother to the Castilians. In 1491, after refusing to surrender the city of Granada to Ferdinand and Isabella, the Castilians laid siege and Boabdil surrendered. Ferdinand's and Isabella's Christian reconquest was complete.

A monastery window at Tomar, Portugal, in the "Manueline" style, combines Gothic fantasy with Italian-Renaissance style.

The Escorial, a palace, monastery, library, and tomb, was built near Madrid for Philip II from 1562. Philip told his architect he wanted "simplicity of form, severity in the whole, nobility without arrogance."

The Golden Age

The Renaissance introduced a golden age in Spain and Portugal. With printed books, often written in national languages, more people could read. The arts flourished, and Spain was, with Italy, one of the first European countries to have professional theaters. Distinctive new styles of architecture used classical motifs. Portugal's greatest poet, Camões (1525–1580), celebrated the Portuguese voyages of discovery in verse.

CENTERS OF LEARNING

MONDOÑEDO
PAMPLONA
BURGOS
GERONA
ZAMORA · VALLADOLID ZARAGOZA LÉRIDA
SALAMANCA EL ESCORIAL SIGÜENZA BARCELONA
· COIMBRA MADRID ALCALÁ DE HENARES TORTOSA
TOLEDO VALENCIA
BAEZA UBEDA MURCIA
SEVILLE GRANADA

📖 Printing centers   ● Universities

Patronage and arts

Besides the Church and the monarchy, rich families such as the Mendozas were patrons of writers and universities. Ferdinand and Isabella attracted German printers to Spain; the Queen herself learned Latin. Salamanca became a centre of European humanism, and in Portugal, João III founded a humanist college at Coimbra.

Italian Influence

Spain and Portugal were strongly influenced by the Italian humanists. They had many contacts with 15th-century Florence, Rome, and Naples (a Spanish possession). Spanish poets wrote in the manner of Petrarch. Portuguese and Spanish scholars translated the classics, and many traveled to Italy and northern Europe.

Just outside the Alhambra, Granada's Moorish palace, Muhammad XI surrenders and bestows upon Isabella and Ferdinand the keys of the city of Granada.

The Spanish humanist philosopher Juan Luis Vives (1492–1540), a friend of Erasmus, tutored English royalty and lectured at Oxford University.

THE GOLDEN AGE

1471
Pope Sixtus IV becomes pope. During his papacy the Spanish Inquisition begins.

1479–1504
Ferdinand of Aragon and Isabella of Castile jointly rule Spain.

1492
Columbus lands in the West Indies; Granada is conquered; Jews expelled from Spain.

1495–1521
Manuel I rules Portugal.

1521–1557
João III rules Portugal.

1556–1598
Philip II rules Spain.

1557–1578
Sebastião rules Portugal. Killed during crusade in Morocco.

1580–1598
Philip II of Spain rules Portugal.

1516–1556
Charles V (Carlos I) rules Spain.

1522
A Spanish ship completes first voyage around the world.

1547
Birth of Cervantes (author of Don Quixote).

1565
Death of Lope de Rueda, Spanish playwright and actor-manager.

1567
Juan de Herrera (1530–1597) becomes architect of the Escorial.

1584
Philip II, admirer of Titian, rejects a picture by El Greco.

Northern Renaissance

The exchange of ideas across Europe was made easier by a common language: Latin, which most educated people could read. The many cultural links between north and south increased in the 15th century. The elegant style in art called "International Gothic" was adopted throughout most of Europe, which, in some ways, was more integrated than it is today.

A Madonna and Child, made to flank an altar, by Rogier van der Weyden.

Dürer's engraving Four Horsemen of the Apocalypse *is a dark Gothic-style vision of Plague, War, Hunger, and Death.*

Here German sculptor Hans Daucher (1486–1538) has used a popular Italian subject: the cupid.

Artistic Tradition

The painters of northern Europe, steeped in the Gothic tradition, were never truly at home with the Italian, classical style. But even before the painters of Florence became famous, Flemish artists such as Jan van Eyck (died 1441) and Rogier van der Weyden (died 1464) were greatly admired in Italy. The most influential German artist was Albrecht Dürer, who also established engraving as a fine art.

The Holy Roman Emperor

The senior European ruler was supposed to be the pope's protector. His actual power was varied. He was king of Germany (at this time a collection of many small states) and had influence in Italy and elsewhere. In the Renaissance, the office was held by the Habsburg Dynasty, who from 1516 also ruled Spain.

The Low Countries and Germany

Besides northern Italy, two other regions in Europe were developing fast in the late Middle Ages. In the Low Countries and Germany, trade, industry, and town life flourished. German cities had considerable independence and no overlord except the emperor, who was usually far away and too busy to interfere. We think of Italy as the birthplace of the Renaissance, but not everything started there. Printing, the most important single development, began in Germany. The technique of painting in oils was perfected in the Netherlands.

One of many portraits of Charles V, emperor and king of Spain, by his court painter and friend, Titian.

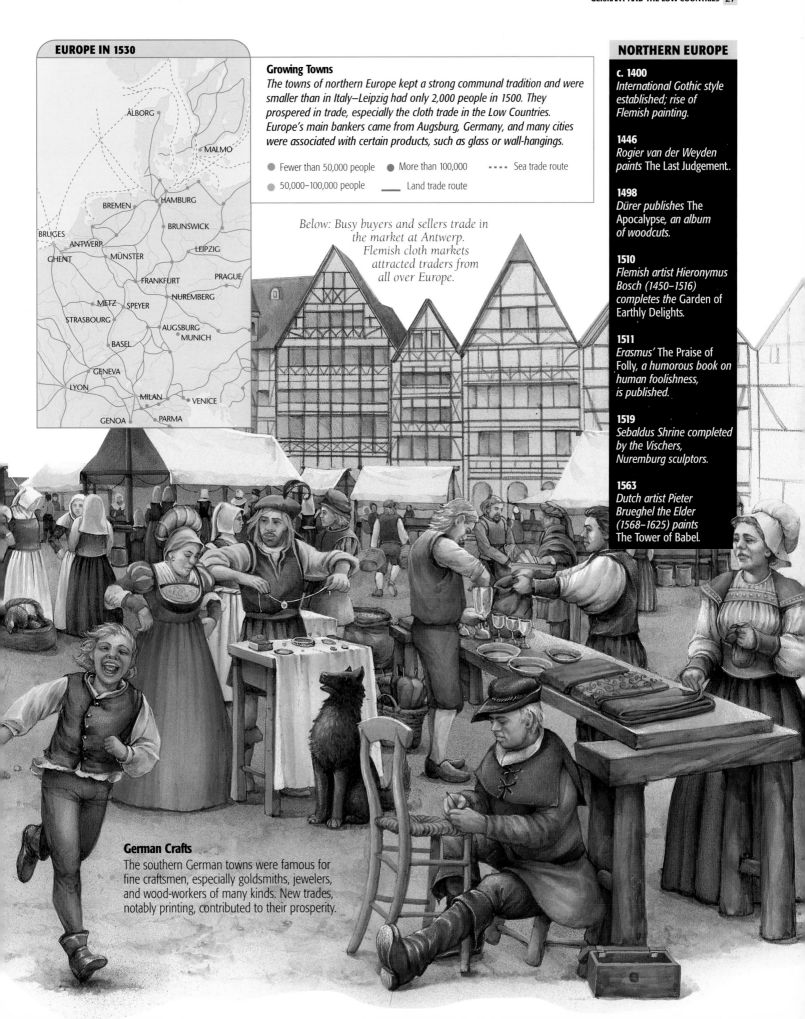

EUROPE IN 1530

ÅLBORG
MALMO
HAMBURG
BREMEN
BRUNSWICK
BRUGES
ANTWERP
GHENT
MÜNSTER
LEIPZIG
FRANKFURT
PRAGUE
METZ
NUREMBERG
SPEYER
STRASBOURG
AUGSBURG
BASEL
MUNICH
GENEVA
LYON
MILAN
VENICE
GENOA
PARMA

Growing Towns

The towns of northern Europe kept a strong communal tradition and were smaller than in Italy–Leipzig had only 2,000 people in 1500. They prospered in trade, especially the cloth trade in the Low Countries. Europe's main bankers came from Augsburg, Germany, and many cities were associated with certain products, such as glass or wall-hangings.

- Fewer than 50,000 people
- More than 100,000
- 50,000–100,000 people
- - - - Sea trade route
- Land trade route

Below: Busy buyers and sellers trade in the market at Antwerp. Flemish cloth markets attracted traders from all over Europe.

NORTHERN EUROPE

c. 1400
International Gothic style established; rise of Flemish painting.

1446
Rogier van der Weyden paints The Last Judgement.

1498
Dürer publishes The Apocalypse, *an album of woodcuts.*

1510
Flemish artist Hieronymus Bosch (1450–1516) completes the Garden of Earthly Delights.

1511
Erasmus' The Praise of Folly, *a humorous book on human foolishness, is published.*

1519
Sebaldus Shrine completed by the Vischers, Nuremburg sculptors.

1563
Dutch artist Pieter Brueghel the Elder (1568–1625) paints The Tower of Babel.

German Crafts

The southern German towns were famous for fine craftsmen, especially goldsmiths, jewelers, and wood-workers of many kinds. New trades, notably printing, contributed to their prosperity.

The Reformation

Christian Europe was deeply religious, yet the Church was unpopular. The Great Schism had weakened the popes, and people were equally dissatisfied with the clergy; many priests and monks were ignorant, dishonest, or greedy. Protests grew. Some reformers challenged the whole establishment of the Catholic Church, including some of its basic beliefs. What began as an effort to reform the Church ended in permanent division and the creation of Protestant churches that rejected the papal authority.

This medal depicts the Dominican pope, Pius V (reigned 1566–1572). Pius brought the sale of indulgences under control and severely punished heresy.

REFORMATION

1517
Pope Leo X encourages sale of indulgences to pay for St. Peter's Cathedral.

1521
Luther condemned by Emperor Charles V.

1524-1525
Peasant rebellions throughout Germany, condemned by Luther.

1531
Protestant German princes form alliance (the League of Schmalkalden).

1534
The king becomes the official head of the English Church.

1536
Calvin's Institutes of the Christian Religion is published.

1555
Peace of Augsburg agrees that a state's religion should be its ruler's.

1560
Scottish parliament adopts Presbyterian (Calvinist) Church.

1572
Massacre of French Protestants (Huguenots) on St Bartholomew's Day.

People who had sinned would buy an indulgence believing it would save them from Hell when they died.

Indulgences

An indulgence was a promise, made on the authority of the Church, that a person's sins would be forgiven. In 1517 papal agents were giving out indulgences on a grand scale in exchange for cash. To reformers, this was just a way of swindling people. Only God could forgive a person's sins, said Martin Luther (1483–1546).

Zwingli and Calvin

The Swiss Ulrich Zwingli (1484–1531) was influenced by Erasmus (a reformer who remained a Catholic). From his headquarters in Zurich, Zwingli had some influence on the future Church of England. John Calvin (1508-1564) was a Frenchman who founded his church in Geneva (1541). Calvinism was severe. It taught that only the "electa" (or "chosen," meaning the Calvinists) would go to Heaven. Calvinist ideas spread widely and strongly influenced French, Dutch and Scottish Protestants.

The Church Divided

The religious division caused several wars. In Germany, a compromise was reached with the Peace of Augsburg (1555). It laid down that every German ruler should decide his own state's religion. Protestantism had advantages for a ruler like the English King Henry VIII (reigned 1509–1547). By rejecting the pope, he gained control of the Church—and its property.

Calvin was the most influential of the Protestant reformers, but Calvinism changed under his successors, who strengthened the idea of God's elect.

RELIGION IN EUROPE IN 1560

SWEDEN
SCOTLAND
IRELAND
DENMARK
ENGLAND
POLAND
HOLY ROMAN EMPIRE
• WITTENBERG
LITHUANIA
FRANCE
IMPERIAL HUNGARY
• AUGSBURG
• GENEVA
OTTOMAN EMPIRE
PAPAL STATES
PORTUGAL
SPAIN

Religious Division

Generally, Protestantism was stronger in northern Europe, Catholicism in the south. Every country contained minorities of different faiths, and in the east, the division was especially close.

- Anglican
- Mixture
- Calvin
- Muslim
- Catholic
- Orthodox
- Lutheran

Here, Luther launches his attack on the Catholic Church. Church doors served as community notice boards.

Martin Luther

In 1517, a Saxon monk named Martin Luther pinned a paper on the church door at Wittenberg listing 95 complaints against the Church. We see this act as the start of the Reformation. When Luther refused to back down, the pope excommunicated him. But he had many supporters in Germany, including the ruler of Saxony. All efforts to reach agreement failed, and the final result was the foundation of a new, Lutheran Church that rejected the Pope and Roman Catholicism.

Protestants rejected the belief that, at holy communion, the bread and wine turn into the body and blood of Jesus.

The Counter-Reformation

At last the Roman Church did reform itself, (though too late to prevent the Reformation), and launched a counter-attack against Protestantism. Strong popes enforced higher standards of behavior among clergy, and supported new, reformed religious orders.

Renaissance Man

We sometimes call a person who is good at several different things a Renaissance man or woman. Work was less specialized in the Renaissance, and an artist might also be a goldsmith, an engineer, an architect, a sculptor, and so on. Michelangelo is famous as a painter and an architect. But he was first of all a sculptor. His 13-foot (4-m) high statue of the biblical character David, done at age 26, demonstrates his mastery of marble.

A detail of Jesus Christ and the Virgin Mary from Michelangelo's The Last Judgement, *the vast painting behind the altar of the Sistine Chapel.*

This altarpiece by German artist Mattias Grünewald (1470–1528) shows a mastery for painting colored light and writhing figures full of emotion.

Leonardo' da Vinci's illustration of the Vitruvian Man *(c. 1490) is a study of the proportions of the human body as described by the ancient Roman architect Vitruvius (1st century BCE).*

High Renaissance Art

The period of Renaissance art lasted for two centuries, from Giotto, the "father of Florentine painting," to Titian, the great Venetian artist. Their styles could hardly be more different. And between them came a great gallery of Renaissance artists, covering a still larger range of styles. The so-called High Renaissance is the period between 1500 and 1527. At that time, classical ideals were strongest, and the best artists had mastered their technique so well that they could paint with perfect accuracy. It was also the period when Rome led the Renaissance, and nearly all the great artists worked there.

Beyond Italy

By the 16th century, the Renaissance had spread to other parts of Europe, although some of its ideas were not always understood in the countries that lacked Italy's classical tradition. Leonardo spent his last years in France. The Florentine sculptor Pietro Torrigiano (1472–1528), famous for breaking Michelangelo's nose in a fight, made his living in England.

Many northern artists visited Rome in the 1520s, and Flemish painters had long been admired in Italy. Great artists active outside Italy during the High Renaissance included Dürer in Germany and Holbein in England.

The Virgin with Child, by German sculptor Tilman Riemenschneider (1460–1531), is at once very naturalistic and deeply mystical.

Leonardo's haunting masterpiece, the Mona Lisa (1505) is of an unknown woman with an enigmatic smile. His "sfumato" technique uses soft outlines and heavy shading.

High Renaissance Painters

Most of Leonardo's works belong to the High Renaissance, along with those of the young Michelangelo and all of Raphael's. These three giants had a huge influence, which still echoes today, although there were others close to them in ability.

A detail from the painting Sacred and Profane Love *by Titian in the style of Giorgione (1477–1510), who was a powerful influence on Titian's early work.*

HIGH RENAISSANCE

c. 1505
Leonardo paints the Mona Lisa.

1508
Michelangelo begins painting the ceiling of the Sistine Chapel.

1512
Dürer is appointed court painter to the Emperor Maximilian I (reigned 1493–1519).

1514
Raphael succeeds Bramante as architect of St. Peter's in Rome.

1514
Andrea del Sarto (1486–1530) paints his fresco, The Birth of the Virgin, *in Florence.*

1518
Titian completes his Assumption, *which begins the High Renaissance.*

1523
Holbein's portraits of Erasmus establish his international reputation.

Renaissance Venice

With Florence and Rome, Venice was the third cultural center of the Renaissance. Venice was safer than most cities and a tolerant place that welcomed foreigners and foreign influences. The outstanding feature of Venetian painting, from Giovanni Bellini (c. 1430–1516) to Titian, was rich and harmonious color.

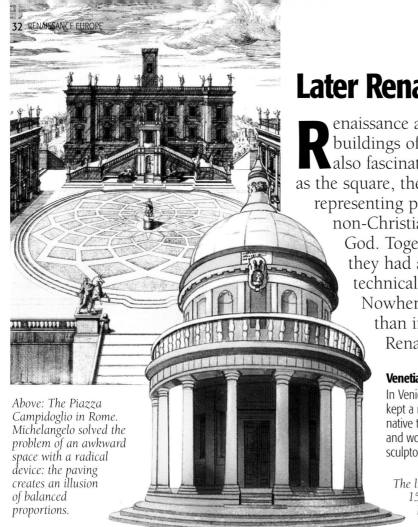

Above: The Piazza Campidoglio in Rome. Michelangelo solved the problem of an awkward space with a radical device: the paving creates an illusion of balanced proportions.

Later Renaissance Architecture

Renaissance architects admired and imitated the buildings of the ancient classical past. They were also fascinated by geometry. They saw forms such as the square, the cube, the circle, and so on, as representing perfection, which for them (unlike the non-Christian ancients) echoed the perfection of God. Together with these powerful influences, they had a quality of their own, which was the technical ability to solve architectural problems. Nowhere was this ability better personified than in the greatest architect of the High Renaissance, Donato Bramante.

Venetian Architecture

In Venice, style changed as it did elsewhere, but the buildings always kept a recognizably Venetian character. Yet many architects were not native to Venice. Jacopo Sansovino (1486–1570) was born in Florence and worked in Rome before settling in Venice in 1527. He began as a sculptor, and his buildings are often highly ornamented with sculpture.

The little "Tempietto," a circular chapel in Rome (begun 1502), is the finest surviving example of Bramante's blend of classical and Renaissance styles.

Donato Bramante

Bramante's reputation rests chiefly on his buildings (including St. Peter's) in Rome, where he arrived at the advanced age of 56. Earlier, he worked in Milan, where he knew Leonardo and shared his interest in buildings on a central plan (for example, a church in the form of a cross with equal arms). Bramante achieved an ideal merging of ancient and modern. He had a genius's understanding of classical principles and, when faced by problems unknown to the ancients, found solutions that were faithful to the classical spirit.

Palladio was the first professional architect. His influence was greatest in the 18th century, long after his death. His Villa Rotonda in Vicenza, Italy, became a model for other European houses built in the classical style.

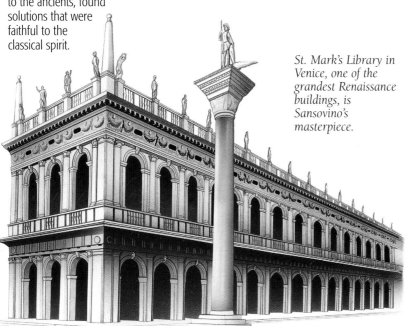

St. Mark's Library in Venice, one of the grandest Renaissance buildings, is Sansovino's masterpiece.

Andrea Palladio

Palladio (1508–1580) learned much from Sansovino, as well as the Romans. Besides churches and palaces, he built many country villas in the Veneto. His houses, which displayed deep understanding of classical principles, were also comfortable and convenient. Palladio's influence rested on his *Four Books of Architecture* (1570), describing his methods, which became a manual of architecture for 200 years. "Palladianism" reached as far as Russia and North America.

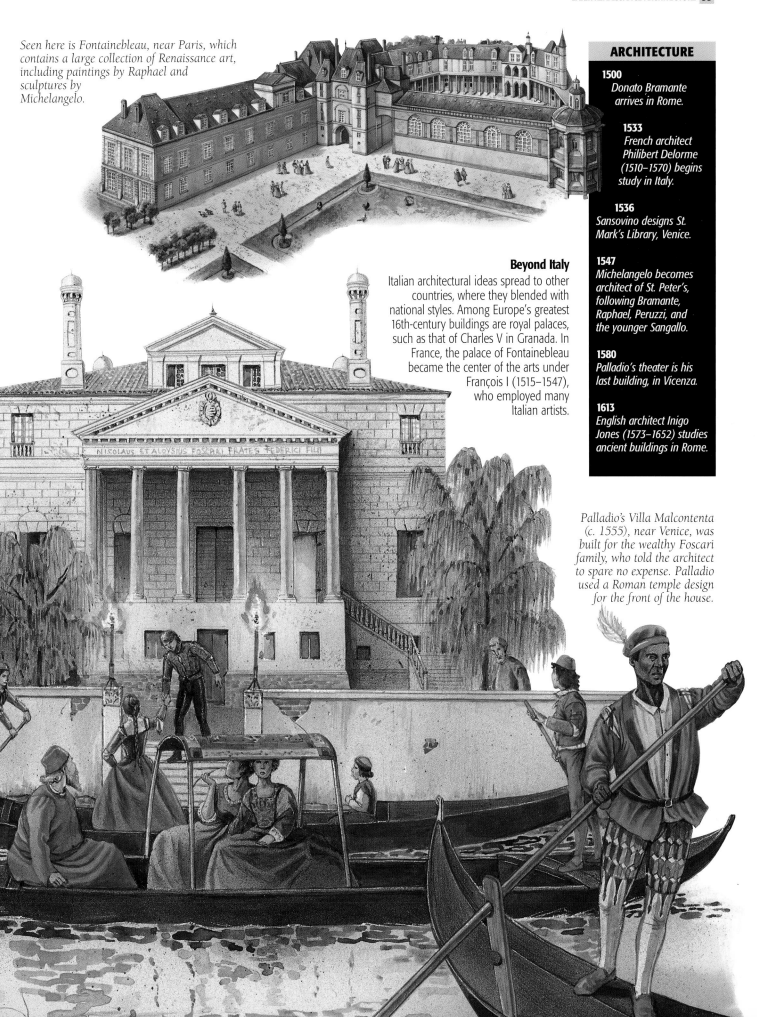

Seen here is Fontainebleau, near Paris, which contains a large collection of Renaissance art, including paintings by Raphael and sculptures by Michelangelo.

ARCHITECTURE

1500
Donato Bramante arrives in Rome.

1533
French architect Philibert Delorme (1510–1570) begins study in Italy.

1536
Sansovino designs St. Mark's Library, Venice.

1547
Michelangelo becomes architect of St. Peter's, following Bramante, Raphael, Peruzzi, and the younger Sangallo.

1580
Palladio's theater is his last building, in Vicenza.

1613
English architect Inigo Jones (1573–1652) studies ancient buildings in Rome.

Beyond Italy

Italian architectural ideas spread to other countries, where they blended with national styles. Among Europe's greatest 16th-century buildings are royal palaces, such as that of Charles V in Granada. In France, the palace of Fontainebleau became the center of the arts under François I (1515–1547), who employed many Italian artists.

Palladio's Villa Malcontenta (c. 1555), near Venice, was built for the wealthy Foscari family, who told the architect to spare no expense. Palladio used a Roman temple design for the front of the house.

Culture and Entertainment

Humanist thinking and books helped raise standards of education. Rising wealth gave privileged men and women more leisure. Love of scholarship and art, based on humanist education, became common. New forms of music were performed: most educated people played a musical instrument. Courts arranged extravagant shows, with music, dancing, and scenic effects. Public theaters were built. There were few organized games. Village folk might play a kind of football, with no rules, and courtiers played tennis.

Gardening became a major art form, often including elaborate fountains. This one at the Farnese Garden in Caprarola near Rome, depicts river gods.

This German candlestick depicts a court jester, a type of clown who was called to lift the spirits of his audience.

Sports

Beside such crude exhibitions as cock-fighting and bear-baiting, most organized sport was connected with hunting or fighting. Jousting (duelling on horseback) was still popular, and provided an opportunity for a carnival, with sideshows and acrobats. Peasants were encouraged to practise archery. The king of France once beat the king of England in a wrestling match.

Seen here are popular amusements, including bull-baiting, in 16th-century Siena.

Ladies playing chess. The pieces took their present-day appearance in the 15th century.

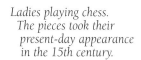

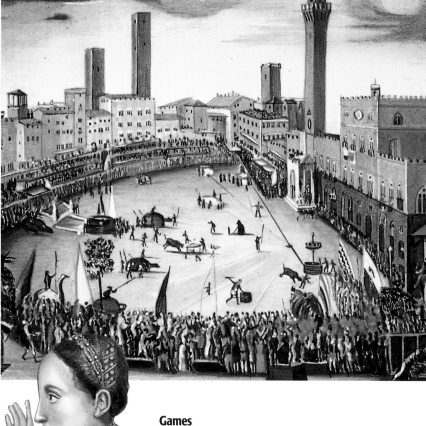

Games

In spite of the rise of professional actors and musicians, most people created their own entertainment. Reading for amusement was a new development. Among old pastimes were indoor board games and cards. People did not have paid holidays, but did have time off at religious festivals and saints' days (holy days), when traveling fairs provided amusements.

Fashion

Clothes, for gentlemen especially, were richer and more decorative than at any other time. Styles varied from year to year, and were usually inspired by Italy. Like art, fashion carried hidden messages no longer easy to understand. In most countries, sumptuary laws dictated what might be worn by people of different social rank.

The grandest clothes and the richest jewelry were worn by the highest class—royalty. Titian painted this fine portrait of Isabella, wife of Emperor Charles V, decked out in her most costly jewels.

Theater and Plays

Early Renaissance plays were performed on temporary stages. The first permanent building was Palladio's theater in Vicenza (1580). New plays, both comedies and tragedies, were written. The famous Italian form of comedy, *commedia dell' arte*, developed in about 1550, partly from court entertainments, partly from street theater.

Before theatres were built, companies of professional actors travelled about, performing in big houses and inn yards.

Music and Dancing

Most Medieval music was religious, but in the Renaissance new forms of music, including songs such as madrigals, were popular everywhere. Printed sheet music let people make their own music at home, and organizations such as trade guilds had their own bands. The beginnings of ballet and opera can be seen in Italian court entertainments toward the end of the 16th century.

A group of 16th-century women playing early instruments, including a recorder, lute, and zither.

Renaissance France

France became a powerful nation-state during the Renaissance. It successfully resisted the English and inherited the provinces of Burgundy, Provence and Brittany. When the French invaded Italy in 1494, they began a long, violent rivalry with the Holy Roman Emperor Charles V, but they also brought France into close contact with the Italian Renaissance. After the death of François I in 1547, France experienced internal religious conflicts, and the kingdom was torn by Catholics fighting Protestants. Yet, 50 years later, France was the greatest power in Europe.

Below: Chambord (completed 1547) is the "fairy-tale" castle of François I and is the largest and best known in the Loire Valley. Designed by an Italian, but built by French stonemasons, it is more French than Italian, and more romantic than classical.

RENAISSANCE CHATEAUX OF THE LOIRE VALLEY

Valley of the Chateaux
This map shows the concentration of 16th-century chateaux (castle-palaces) in France's Loire Valley. Many were built as hunting lodges, and François I owned eight of the largest. Progress was cut short by the religious wars.

François I
Intelligent, dashing and extravagant, François I admired the culture of the Italian Renaissance and was himself the model of a Renaissance prince. He increased the power and wealth of the monarchy and was a keen patron of the arts, spending a fortune hiring Italian artists to work on ambitious projects such as Chambord.

Portrait of François I, patron of many artists, including Leonardo da Vinci.

A detail of a painting by a Fontainebleau artist showing the Colosseum in Rome.

Enamel from Fontainebleau representing the ancient Greek god Apollo.

The School of Fontainebleau

At the heart of the French Renaissance was the royal palace of Fontainebleau, which gave its name to a school of art, inspired by classicism and noted for decorative plasterwork and wood carving. Its founder, the Florentine Rosso Fiorentino, known as "Il Rosso"(1494–1540), was one of many Italians working there.

Above: The title page of Gargantua, a satire by François Rabelais (1494–1553), which paints a lively picture of France in the early 16th century.

Upon seeing this extravagant gold saltcellar made by the Italian artist Benvenuto Cellini (1500–1571), the king exclaimed that it was one of the most "divine" objects he had ever seen.

Humanism and Literature

Literature, not painting, was the outstanding art of Renaissance France, encouraged by the spread of humanist thought and the printing revolution. Its leading figure, one of the greatest in all French literature, was Rabelais, humanist scholar and creator of the stories of *Gargantua* and *Pantagruel*. Pierre de Ronsard (1524–1585) was the leader of a group of poets, the *Pléiade*, who wrote in the style of Petrarch. Michel de Montaigne (1533–1592) in his library tower composed beautiful and original essays. These and other writers contributed to the vigorous growth of the modern French language.

This figure was used to teach anatomy. Knowledge of how the body is made was greatly advanced during the Renaissance.

Jars like these were used by pharmacies to store herbs and medicine.

In this detail of a work by Raphael (1511), the great Greek geometrist Euclid (3rd century BCE) explains his ideas at Plato's Academy in Athens.

Medicine

No one knew how the body worked or how diseases were caused, and they had no drugs to treat them. Herbs were widely used, and sometimes worked, but doctors were groping in the dark. An intelligent doctor recommended fresh air and exercise, but he could not explain why those things were good for people. He had simply noticed their good effect.

Engineering and Mathematics

The greatest technical advance was printing. Other inventions, like the machines drawn by Leonardo, were limited by lack of power: no form of engine, or motor, existed. Knowledge of mathematics also advanced. Leonardo probably learned his maths from Luca Pacioli (died c. 1520), whose book on arithmetic contained the first description of double-entry book-keeping (essential for keeping business accounts).

Hospitals and Apothecaries

All hospitals were charities, run by monasteries or supported by rich people. They provided rest and care, but seldom a cure. Most doctors avoided them. An apothecary was the forerunner of a chemist or pharmacist. He made or traded in medicines. Apothecaries often acted as doctors.

Portrait of Luca Pacioli, who wrote books on mathematics, including one on geometry illustrated by Leonardo.

Science and Medicine

In the Middle Ages, science as we know it did not exist. People's knowledge of the natural world was based on folklore, superstition, and religious teaching. The ancient Greeks had understood the world much better, and the first step towards modern science was to recover the ancient texts and study Greek learning. However, even the Greeks' science was limited. Although they based their ideas on reason, they did few scientific experiments. The next step was to advance beyond the Greeks through observation and experiment.

Astronomy

The chief authority on astronomy and geography was Ptolemy, a Greek who lived in the 2nd century CE. He taught that the Earth is the center of the universe and does not move. A Polish scholar, Nicolaus Copernicus (1473–1543), having read other Greek thinkers who disagreed with Ptolemy, published a book in 1543 explaining that the Earth moves around the Sun. His theory was condemned by the Church, and few people believed it until the 17th century.

Here, alchemists practise their craft. Among other things, they hoped to find an "elixir" that would prolong life indefinitely and a universal remedy for every ill.

Alchemy and Astrology

Alchemists practised an unscientific form of chemistry. They based their work on supposed authorities, but their ideas were governed by religious or magic beliefs. For example, they believed it was possible to turn ordinary metal into gold. Astrology, the belief that the stars influence human affairs, was also popular, and still is today!

Copernicus' calculations showed that the movement of the planets could be best explained if the Earth moved around the Sun. It was a great scientific breakthrough.

A copy of Copernicus' On the Revolution of Heavenly Bodies *(1543).*

A mid-16th century celestial sphere from Florence. The metal rings of the sphere represent the equator, the tropics and the Arctic and Antarctic circles.

England and Scotland

Renaissance influences came to Britain, and especially to Scotland, largely through France, Scotland's ally. Although the influence of the Renaissance could be seen before 1500, the principles of classical architecture and art were little understood until early 17th century. England, like France, became a powerful, centralized monarchy in this period. Adoption of a state religion further strengthened the monarchy. Scotland also became a Protestant country, after a long, bitter struggle.

Leading English Protestants were burned at the stake as heretics under the Catholic Mary I, known as "Bloody Mary" (reigned 1553–1558).

The Reformation in Britain

The papacy's authority in England ended after the pope refused to allow King Henry VIII a divorce. Henry made himself head of the English Church in 1532, which turned Protestant under his son Edward VI, Catholic again during the reign of his daughter Mary I, and Protestant finally under Elizabeth I. Calvin's follower John Knox led the Scottish Reformation, establishing the Presbyterian Church in 1560.

Renaissance Princes

Henry VIII was England's equivalent to France's François I. Scotland's "Renaissance prince" was King James IV (reigned 1513–1542). Both were handsome and intelligent, fond of music, patrons of the arts, builders of palaces, and supporters of scholarship. But England's "golden age" began later, in about 1580, during the reign of Henry VIII's second daughter, Elizabeth I.

Intellectuals

The chief centers of learning outside London were the universities of Oxford and Cambridge, where humanism was encouraged by Italian visitors. Erasmus lectured at Oxford and was a friend of the English humanist, Sir Thomas More (1477–1535), author of *Utopia* (a description of an ideal society). Scotland had three universities, but in the older, Medieval tradition.

In painting Sir Thomas More, Hans Holbein achieved a degree of realism and delicacy of touch unprecedented in England at the time.

This finely painted miniature of a handsome young nobleman (1587) was of a type fashionable during the Elizabethan period.

The Elizabethan Age

As in France, England's greatest cultural achievement of the 16th century was in literature. Besides Hans Holbein, a German, there were few great painters, and portraits were their only subject. In music, the English eagerly adopted the madrigal from Italy. Composers included Thomas Tallis, his pupil William Byrd, and John Dowland. Building public theaters brought opportunities to a brilliant generation of poet-playwrights, including William Shakespeare (1564–1616).

The Queen's House in Greenwich, by Inigo Jones (1573–1652), England's first professional architect. He introduced the classical style from Italy.

Mary Queen of Scots

Elizabeth I's cousin Mary became queen of Scotland in 1542 after living in France since childhood. She brought French, Catholic influence to Scotland, but her behavior irritated her subjects, who rebelled. Mary fled to England, where Elizabeth kept her prisoner. When Catholics plotted to put her on the English throne, she was executed as a traitor in 1587.

This brooch with Mary's portrait probably belonged to one of her supporters.

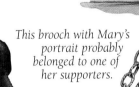

King Henry VIII is here seated majestically between his daughter Mary and her husband Philip II of Spain (left), and his son Edward and second daughter Elizabeth (right).

BRITAIN

1476
William Caxton sets up the first English press.

1509–1547
Henry VIII rules England. Art and literature encouraged.

1513
Scots James IV is killed in English victory of Flodden.

1533
Parliament passes the Act of Appeals, ending pope's authority in England.

1553–1558
Reign of Mary I, who restores Catholicism.

1555
John Knox returns to Scotland and attacks Catholic influence.

1558–1603
Elizabeth I rules: England's Golden Age.

1563
The Church of England established by the Thirty-Nine Articles.

ENGLAND AND SCOTLAND IN 1598

Three Churches

By 1598 the British Isles were divided among three distinct churches. The Church of England (Anglican Church), dominated England. Scotland's more severe brand of Protestantism modelled itself on Calvinism. In Ireland Protestantism and Catholicism co-existed in a situation that has caused unrest to the present day.

- Mainly Calvinist
- Mainly Anglican
- Mainly Catholic

SCOTLAND
IRELAND
DUBLIN
YORK
ENGLAND
CAMBRIDGE
OXFORD
LONDON

NORTHERN AND EASTERN EUROPE IN 1550

STOCKHOLM •

LITHUANIA

• MOSCOW   KAZAN

HOLY
ROMAN
EMPIRE

• WARSAW

• CRACOW   ASTRAKHAN

• PRAGUE

The ancient island-castle of Kalmar, Sweden, was largely reconstructed in Renaissance style in the 16th century. It contains beautiful rooms, such as the chamber of King Eric XXIV.

Russia, Poland, and Sweden

By this time, the small medieval duchy of Muscovy had become the large and expanding empire of Russia. Sweden had gained independence from Denmark. Poland reached its greatest territorial extent. But large stretches of eastern Europe remained forested or swampy, with few people and little farming or industry.

- Denmark and Norway
- Sweden
- Poland
- Russia
- Austria and Hungary

St. Basil's church in Moscow commemorates Ivan IV's victory over the Tatars. Russian art followed a national tradition, but was influenced by Byzantium.

Scandinavia

In Scandinavia, too, the peasants were squeezed and the monarchy weak compared with the nobility and the German merchants who controlled trade. Things changed after 1523, when Gustavus Vasa became king of Sweden. He made the monarchy hereditary (1544), introduced Protestantism and began to make Sweden a major European power.

Portrait of Gustavus Vasa (reigned 1523–1560), the first of Sweden's Vasa Dynasty.

Northern and Eastern Europe

At the time of the Renaissance, the north and east of Europe were still fairly backward, with different cultural traditions. In the west, most peasants were given their freedom, and nation-states were forming under strong, hereditary monarchs. In the east the opposite was happening, with peasants becoming serfs—slaves owned by landowners. Most eastern kings were elected. As a result, they could not control their powerful native nobles. Government was weak.

This illustration from a book of the 16th century shows the sejm, the Polish parliament.

Bohemia

The Habsburg emperor Rudolf II (reigned 1576–1612) moved his court from Vienna to Prague, the capital of Bohemia, in 1576. A learned man, he made the city a major center of culture. He invited artists, writers, and scientists to his court, including the astronomer Johannes Kepler (1571–1630), who discovered the laws governing the movement of the planets.

Rudolf II by his court painter Giuseppe Arcimboldo (1527–1593), famous for making faces out of fruits and vegetables.

Poland

Poland, combined with Lithuania, was the largest kingdom in Europe. In about 1500, a Renaissance monarchy was developing. The court was a center of Italian art, Italian artists rebuilt the Wawel castle in Renaissance style and Cracow was known for humanist scholarship. But the selfishness of the nobles, Poland's lack of a town-based middle class, and its weak monarchy, especially after the Jagiellon Dynasty ended in 1572, prevented further development.

Transforming Russia

Russia was an exception to the rest of eastern and northern Europe. A powerful monarchy emerged under Ivan III, who took the title tsar (emperor). Russia was heavily influenced by Byzantium, the old Eastern Roman Empire. It was not Roman Catholic, but Greek Orthodox, and the great national task of the tsars was to drive the Tatars back into Central Asia. Ivan III employed Italians to rebuild Moscow and the Kremlin, but Renaissance thinking had little effect.

This late 16th-century ceremonial musket was made for an Austrian archduke.

Warfare

War was a normal part of life during the Renaissance. The states of Europe were themselves created by wars, and most men not in holy orders were part-time soldiers. Wars were fought for power and territory, as well as for freedom and religion. This period brought great changes in warfare, mostly the result of technological advances. By 1500, gunpowder cannon were becoming much more powerful and accurate.

Portrait of the great Italian condottiere *Muzio Attendolo Sforza.*

Above: A watchtower is defended by cannon, which could be moved around to fire in any direction.

Weapons and Defence

Guns enabled European ships to control ocean trade routes. They made stone castles and knights' armor less effective, and only exceptionally strong castles could resist cannon. New castles were rounded (not square) to deflect shot. Hand-guns were still inaccurate, slow to reload, likely to explode in your face and no good in the rain.

Armies

Renaissance armies were often made up of mercenaries, especially in Italy. A successful *condottiere,* or commander of mercenaries, could gain power and wealth. Muzio Attendoli (1369–1424), nicknamed "Sforza" ("Strength"), was born a peasant, became a *condottiere* and, later, founder of the Sforza Dynasty of Milan.

Warrior Kings

The earliest kings were tribal war leaders, and Renaissance kings still led their armies in battle. The greatest contest was between the kings of France and the Habsburg emperors, who also led Christian resistance against attack by Ottoman Turks. The Emperor Charles V wisely advised his successor to avoid war, as it caused great misery and was so expensive it could ruin the state.

The Florentine statesman and writer Niccolò Machiavelli (1469–1527) in his work, The Prince *(1532), describes how "good arms" are necessary for "good laws." He also stated that mercenary soldiers were dangerous since they were not loyal.*

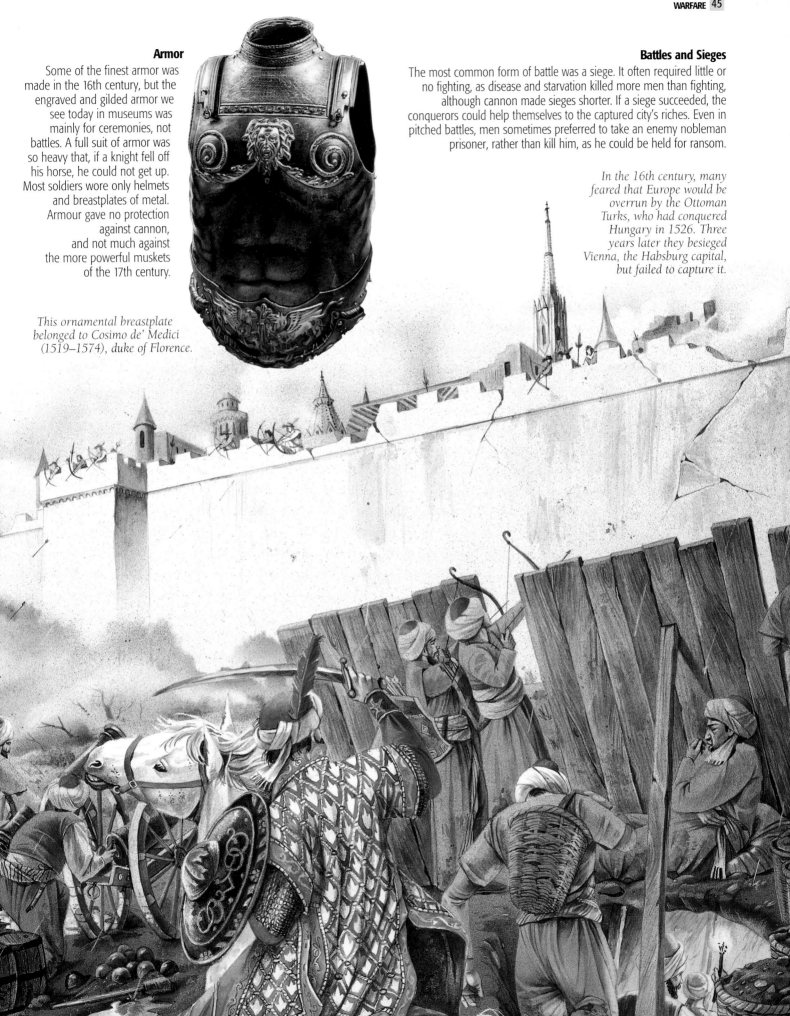

Armor

Some of the finest armor was made in the 16th century, but the engraved and gilded armor we see today in museums was mainly for ceremonies, not battles. A full suit of armor was so heavy that, if a knight fell off his horse, he could not get up. Most soldiers wore only helmets and breastplates of metal. Armour gave no protection against cannon, and not much against the more powerful muskets of the 17th century.

This ornamental breastplate belonged to Cosimo de' Medici (1519–1574), duke of Florence.

Battles and Sieges

The most common form of battle was a siege. It often required little or no fighting, as disease and starvation killed more men than fighting, although cannon made sieges shorter. If a siege succeeded, the conquerors could help themselves to the captured city's riches. Even in pitched battles, men sometimes preferred to take an enemy nobleman prisoner, rather than kill him, as he could be held for ransom.

In the 16th century, many feared that Europe would be overrun by the Ottoman Turks, who had conquered Hungary in 1526. Three years later they besieged Vienna, the Habsburg capital, but failed to capture it.

Glossary

Altarpiece A religious painting that sits at the back of a church altar.

Alchemy An unscientific method of chemistry that involved seeking a way of turning base metals into gold and producing a universal remedy for all illnesses.

Amphitheater An open-air building, usually round or oval, with seating constructed for the viewing of sporting events or other spectacles taking place in the center of the structure.

Anatomy The study of the structure of a plant or animal, especially of the human body.

Apothecaries A historical name for pharmacists or doctors. During the Renaissance apothecaries were respected for their knowledge of herbal remedies for illnesses. They also performed surgery.

Baptistry The part of a church were baptisms are carried out, usually near the front door. This is to symbolize a person's spiritual entry into the life of the Church.

Calvinism A more severe form of Protestantism named after John Calvin (1509–1564), leader of the Reformation in France and Switzerland.

Chapel A small place of Christian worship that is usually attached to a larger building, such as a cathedral, monastery, fortress, or castle.

City-state In northern Italy during the Renaissance, an independent city that governed itself through a council or ruling family.

Classical Refers to the civilizations of ancient Greece and Rome, and, in particular their culture, art, and architecture.

Commission To employ an artist, builder, or craftsman to create something. During the Renaissance commissions were handed out by wealthy people who were called patrons.

Condottiere The commander of a troop of mercenary soldiers in Europe from the 13th to the 16th centuries. *Condottieri* were renowned for their skill with the crossbow.

Doge Name given to the ruler of the Republic of Venice. Various 16th-century doges were great patrons of Renaissance artists and architects.

Dynasty A line of rulers coming from the same family, or a period during which they reign.

Florin A gold coin minted in Florence and which became a standard currency throughout Europe during the 15th century.

Foreshortening A perspective trick in painting. An example would be where a picture creates an illusion of an arm pointing directly at the viewer. In fact, only the hand is shown; the arm is hidden behind the hand.

Fresco A picture painted onto a wall while the plaster is still damp. The paint binds to the plaster as it dries and the image becomes part of the wall.

Feudal system The social system that existed in western Europe in early Medieval times in which peasants worked on the land of their local lord in return for his protection. The peasants also had to fight as soldiers if required by their lord.

Gothic The style of European art before the Renaissance, from the 12th to the 15th centuries. Its main feature in architecture was the soaring, pointed arch.

Guild A group of people usually belonging to the same trade or profession, who unite in an organization to protect their common interests. Guilds were also patrons of artists, sculptors, and buildings.

Heresy An opinion that differs from the official teachings of the Church.

Humanism The idea that humans can improve by their own efforts and by reason, rather than through religion or the teachings of the Church.

Inquisition A jury of the Roman Catholic Church set up to root out and punish heresy.

Medieval Something that relates to the Middle Ages.

Middle Ages A period of European history from about the 5th century to the 14th century. The Renaissance followed the Middle Ages.

Miniature A very small, finely painted picture, usually a portrait. The word comes from the Latin "minimum," meaning the red lead used to make the red ink in Medieval illuminated manuscripts.

Monopolise To have complete control over something without competition from anyone else. For example, during the Renaissance the guilds often had a monopoly on the practise of their craft or trade.

Moveable type The small reusable metal letters that were used in the early printing presses. They were the key technology that spread the Renaissance in the 15th century through the production and distribution of printed books.

Mural A picture painted directly onto a wall.

Perspective A method of showing three-dimensional distance in a two-dimensional picture, using techniques such as making distant objects in the scene look smaller than those that are closer.

Pioneer Someone who leads the way in developing something new and original.

Plague An infectious disease, usually with a high death rate. The plague known as the Black Death spread from Asia during the 14th century and killed about 50 million people in Europe. Infection was spread by fleas carried on rats.

Reformation The religious and political movement of the 16th century that began as an attempt by churches in northern Europe to reform the Roman Catholic Church. The Reformation resulted in the establishment of the Protestant churches, which denied the authority of the pope.

Renaissance A movement in the arts, literature, and science in which a rediscovery of the classical cultures of the ancient world led to a rebirth of culture. It involved developments such as greater realism in painting and sculpture. It began in 14th-century Italy and spread throughout Europe.

Renaissance man A man who is highly gifted in several different fields of study, particularly in both arts and sciences. The ability to master several fields was an ideal of the Renaissance.

Rotunda A building or a room with a circular plan, especially one that has a dome.

Secular A term referring to something non-religious.

"Sfumato" A style of painting such as that used by Leonardo da Vinci in his *Mona Lisa*. Outlines are painted softly and the shading is very dark.

Theological Something that relates to the study of God's existence and all things holy or divine.

Vellum A type of smooth writing paper made from calfskin.

Index